W9-BXQ-175

Also by Charlotte Foltz Jones

Mistakes That Worked:
40 Familiar Inventions and How They Came to Be

Accidents May Happen:
50 Inventions Discovered by Mistake

Fingerprints and Talking Bones:
How Real-Life Crimes Are Solved

YUKON GOLD

YUKON GOLD

The Story of the Klondike Gold Rush

CHARLOTTE FOLTZ JONES

Holiday House / NEW YORK

Library of Congress Cataloging-in-Publication Data
Jones, Charlotte Foltz.
Yukon gold : the story of the Klondike Gold Rush /
Charlotte Foltz Jones.—1st ed.
p. cm.
Includes bibliographical references and index.
Summary: Recounts the quest for gold that took place in the late
1890s in the Klondike region of the Yukon Territory of
northwestern Canada.
ISBN 0–8234–1403–5 (hardcover : alk. paper)
1. Klondike River Valley (Yukon)—Gold discoveries—Juvenile
literature. [1. Klondike River Valley (Yukon)—Gold discoveries.]
I. Title.
F1095.K5J66 1998 98-20977 CIP AC
971.9' 1—dc21

Map copyright © 1999 by David Lindroth, Inc.

For
John R. Imig, M.D.
Peter C. Ewing, M.D.
Patrick L. Moran, M.D.
Allen B. Dunning, M.D.

—who know about survival

With special thanks to
Mary Cash, for her faith
Bill Jones, for his steadfastness

The author also wishes to acknowledge the assistance of
India Spartz and the staff at the Alaska State Library
Denver Public Library, Western History Department staff
Carolyn J. Marr, Museum of History and Industry
National Park Service
Seattle Post-Intelligencer
Richard H. Engeman, University of Washington, Special Collections
Marjorie Kevlahan and Susan Camilleri, Vancouver Public Library
Elaine Miller, Washington State Historical Society
Peggy D'Orsay and the staff of the Yukon Archives

TABLE OF CONTENTS

YUKON GOLD

CHAPTER 1

———◆—◆◆◆—

AMERICA NEEDED A MIRACLE

Gold!

The word is electrifying. Even in a world where most of us see gold only in jewelry or as a decoration on our mother's dishes, *gold* still stirs excitement and visions of great wealth.

But a century ago, gold was magical. It could turn a poor person into a millionaire, and there were many poor people.

The economy of the United States fell into a depression in 1893. In this "Panic of 1893," 156 railroads claimed bankruptcy, 15,000 businesses failed, and 642 banks closed, wiping out the savings of thousands of people. One quarter of the country's industries stopped production. Four million people out of a population of 65 million could not get jobs. A man felt lucky if he could get work for a day or two.

Today there are welfare programs for unemployed people, but one hundred years ago there was no help. There were few jobs and thousands of people had no money to buy food or pay the rent. Stores closed because customers could not afford to buy their goods.

People lost hope. Some people starved to death. Many committed suicide. Others went crazy.

With so much hardship, people dreamed of instant wealth and would do anything to get rich in a hurry. The vision of thousands of dollars in gold was captivating.

When people can't find jobs, they get restless. They believe there is opportunity "somewhere else" and all they have to do is get "there." So when stories of gold spread, it was easy for people to catch "gold fever."

The people who joined the rush for gold had been waiting for a miracle. When the steamships *Excelsior* and *Portland* docked in San Francisco and Seattle, it seemed that their miracle had arrived.

CHAPTER 2

WHERE IS THE KLONDIKE?

Once the gold rush began, people headed north. But most of them had no clear idea where Alaska or the Yukon or the Klondike was.

The Yukon was a river and a territory of Canada.

The Klondike was a river and a region that encompassed a section of Alaska and a section of the Yukon Territory of Canada.

The United States purchased the 365 million acres of Alaska from Russia in 1867 for $7.2 million. But in 1897 the boundaries between the United States and Canada had yet to be clearly drawn.

The gold seekers didn't really care whether they found their gold in Alaska or in Canada. They just wanted to get there and get their share.

Getting to the Goldfields

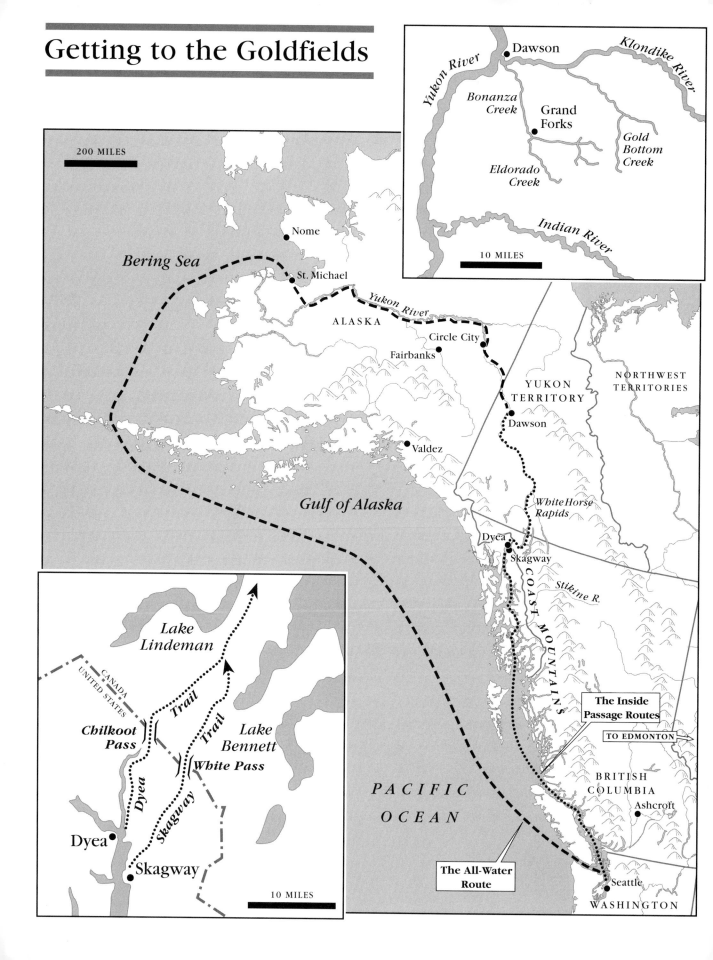

200 MILES

Bering Sea

Nome

St. Michael

ALASKA

Yukon River

Circle City

Fairbanks

Valdez

Gulf of Alaska

YUKON TERRITORY

NORTHWEST TERRITORIES

Dawson

White Horse Rapids

Dyea

Skagway

COAST MOUNTAINS

Stikine R.

PACIFIC OCEAN

The Inside Passage Routes

TO EDMONTON

BRITISH COLUMBIA

Ashcroft

The All-Water Route

Seattle

WASHINGTON

Yukon River

Dawson

Klondike River

Bonanza Creek

Grand Forks

Gold Bottom Creek

Eldorado Creek

Indian River

10 MILES

Lake Lindeman

CANADA
UNITED STATES

Trail

Chilkoot Pass

Trail

Lake Bennett

White Pass

Dyea

Dyea

Skagway

Skagway

10 MILES

CHAPTER 3

———◆———

THE YUKON
BEFORE THE GOLD RUSH

After the California gold rush in 1849, prospectors searched for gold all over the West—in Oregon, Washington, Montana, Arizona, Nevada, Colorado, Idaho, South Dakota, and British Columbia.

Explorers mapped and charted Alaska. Trappers and traders gathered furs. Missionaries built missions. And prospectors searched for gold.

Trading posts were built in the Yukon. Towns were established. In the summer of 1895, the town called Forty Mile (named because of its distance from old Fort Reliance) had a population of about 260. There were at least a thousand non-natives in the Yukon Valley. Five hundred more arrived before the end of the summer in 1896.

The prospectors were not affected by the terrible economy Outside (as the miners called the rest of the civilized world). They had no telephones, no telegraphs, and the few newspapers that arrived were usually six to nine months old.

Did they care?

Most of these prospectors liked their lifestyle. They panned for gold along the creeks and streams, always hoping for the "mother lode." They lived off the land and carried a rucksack of life's bare essentials: a gold pan, a pick and shovel, some beans, bacon, and tea. There was one more necessity: a crock of sourdough. Sourdough is fermented dough. Mixed with extra flour and water, it makes biscuits or flapjacks rise without yeast or baking soda. Because the old prospectors cooked with sourdough, they became known as sourdoughs.

Many prospectors had nicknames, too, like Jimmy the Pirate, Tom the Horse, Happy Jack, Salt Water Jack, Calamity Bill, Dirty Joe, French Curly, Hootchinoo Albert, and Pete the Pig.

Prospectors who had been in the North for a long time were called sourdoughs. These two are making sourdough flapjacks.

Most of the miners walked wherever they wanted to go. They had no time schedules, no appointments, no deadlines, and no need to hurry.

If they had more than they could carry, they used sleds pulled by dogs. But the dogs had tremendous appetites, and it cost about three dollars a day to feed each dog. The number of dogs needed to pull a sled varied by how much the sled weighed. Many dog teams had six or seven dogs, but even one good dog could pull three hundred pounds.

The few women who lived in the northlands were treated with respect by the miners. A lady named Mrs. Wills went north in 1895. She was determined to support her disabled husband. She staked a claim and then baked bread and sold it for a dollar a loaf until she'd saved $230 to buy a washtub, a washboard, a box of starch, and a supply of wood to heat

Many women made money by washing clothes for the miners.

the water. She then began doing miners' laundry. With her laundry earnings, she paid laborers to work her claim. She was soon worth more than $250,000.

If a miner wanted a bath, there was a bathhouse in town—a small tent with a stove inside. For $1.50, he could get five minutes in a wooden laundry tub.

Other than saloons, dance halls, and gambling, the miners had little entertainment. There was an occasional squaw dance when the native women came into town and danced with the miners. Some towns had a literary society where the miners discussed Shakespeare, poetry, science, or philosophy. Miners also met in roadhouses, which were gathering places close to the diggings.

This roadhouse was on the Yukon River. Roadhouses were anything from a tent with crates for chairs to a hotel with a dining room and sleeping quarters.

A miner might prospect for years without finding enough gold even to pay his expenses. Most trading-post operators believed gold would be found in their region if enough prospectors kept searching. To encourage the men to keep looking, the trading-post operators would "grubstake" prospectors— sometimes for years.

By the end of each winter, when trading-post supplies ran short, the post operators distributed food equally, even to prospectors who could not pay. It was an unwritten code that no one should starve just because his claim was not paying.

The mining camps made their own laws. One law was honesty. A miner would never steal his neighbor's belongings. If a miner built a cabin away from civilization, he never locked it. If he was gone, someone coming upon his cabin could go inside to sleep or escape the weather. Anyone using a cabin was expected to clean up after himself, replace the firewood he used, and replace the food he ate when he was able to do so.

In town, gold dust was kept in buckskin sacks with the owner's name on it. The bags were stacked on a shelf behind the bar in the saloon or under the counter at the trading post.

Once when a shipment of goods arrived at Arthur Harper's trading post, the miners were impatient to get their supplies. Harper told them to take what they needed and keep track of what they took. They could settle up later. When all the accounts were paid, only six cans of condensed milk were not paid for. And that could have been an error made when the cargo was shipped.

The unwritten code of honesty would change once the Klondike gold rush began.

CHAPTER 4

DISCOVERY

One man called it "the biggest thing in the world." He was talking about the beginning of the Klondike gold rush.

There are several stories of the discovery of the gold. It started with four men—Robert Henderson, George Washington Carmack, Tagish Charlie, and Skookum Jim—and some hard feelings.

Robert Henderson had grown up in Nova Scotia and had searched for gold in New Zealand, Australia, and Colorado before he went north to the Yukon in 1894. In the early summer of 1896, he found a pan of gold worth eight cents in a creek he named Gold Bottom. That was considered a good prospect. By the middle of the summer, Henderson and some other prospectors had taken out $750 worth of gold. That was more than some people earned in an entire year.

Henderson went into the town of Ogilvie about the middle of July 1896 to buy supplies. To return to his camp, he took the Klondike River. That was where he saw George Carmack, a white man who had adopted the natives' lifestyle and taken a wife of the Tagish tribe.

Carmack was camped with Tagish Charlie and Skookum

Robert Henderson

Tagish Charlie

George Carmack

Skookum Jim

Jim, his wife's relatives, at the mouth of the Klondike River where it flowed into the Yukon River. The men were fishing and cutting logs to sell to a sawmill.

Henderson told of finding gold in the nearby creek. There was an unwritten code among the prospectors: When someone found an unusual amount of gold, he shared the good news with other prospectors. And that's what Henderson did.

Carmack said that Tagish Charlie, Skookum Jim, and he would come over to Gold Bottom and stake some claims. Henderson objected, saying Carmack was welcome, but he didn't want the creek staked by the natives, whom the miners called Siwash.

Carmack and his relatives did not like Henderson's insult.

Henderson left and returned to his diggings.

About three weeks later Carmack, Tagish Charlie, and Skookum Jim went over to Gold Bottom to see if the gold looked promising. When they met up with Henderson, their provisions were low. Tagish Charlie and Skookum Jim offered to pay Henderson well for some tobacco, but Henderson would not sell them any.

The three left for Rabbit Creek. They were almost out of provisions, and they were hungry. Skookum Jim went ahead of the others and shot a moose. While waiting for Carmack and Tagish Charlie to catch up so that they could cook it, Jim went down to the creek to get a drink. There he saw gold—more gold than he had ever seen in one place. When he showed Carmack and Tagish Charlie, Carmack later said, "We did a war dance around that pan: a combination Scottish horn-pipe, Indian fox trot, syncopated Irish jig, and Siwash hula-hula."

The three men panned the creek for two days, deciding

where to stake their claims. In one pan, they found four dollars' worth of gold—the most anyone had ever found in a single pan in the Klondike region.

They disagreed about who should file the Discovery claim. This was important, since whoever filed the Discovery claim was entitled to stake an additional claim—a total of two claims. Everyone else could stake only one claim in a mining district.

Carmack finally overruled Skookum Jim. He said that since Jim was a native, he could not record a Discovery claim *and* an adjoining claim. This was not entirely true, but Jim and Carmack finally reached an agreement: On August 17, 1896, Carmack shared the Discovery claim with Jim. Carmack, Tagish Charlie, and Skookum Jim staked adjoining claims.

Each claim stretched five hundred feet along the creek and was as wide as the valley, from the base of the hill on one side to the base of the hill on the other side of the creek.

Once the claims were staked, Jim stayed behind while Carmack and Tagish Charlie took logs downriver to the sawmill at the town of Forty Mile. They also recorded their claims at the police post.

As was the custom, Carmack shared the good news of his find with other miners. But many of the old-timers had no respect for Carmack. They called him Lyin' George.

Carmack showed them a shotgun-shell casing filled with gold. As the Canadian government surveyor William Ogilvie said, "The gold in the shell casing had to come from somewhere!" By the next morning, the town of Forty Mile was deserted.

Carmack and Tagish Charlie returned to their claims. Within days the miners changed the name of Rabbit Creek to a more appropriate name: Bonanza Creek.

The Bonanza Creek valley did not "look like" a place to find gold. The old sourdoughs looked for certain things: The willows leaned a certain way. The water had a certain taste. And the moose didn't graze where there was gold. This valley was too wide. It was on the wrong side of the Yukon. The willows were wrong; the water was wrong; and it was a moose pasture. But the gold was there.

Locally, the news spread quickly. By the middle of September 1896, prospectors had filed 200 claims on Bonanza Creek. By November 20, 338 claims had been recorded and another 150 were being processed.

As more prospectors came to stake claims, a richer discovery was made on a creek named Eldorado. (*El Dorado* is a Spanish term referring to a place of great riches and treasures.) One claim on Eldorado Creek yielded a pan worth $212.

Carmack did not send word to Henderson about the discovery. Although Henderson was working just on the other side of the mountain, he did not learn of the big discovery until much later. By then, Bonanza and Eldorado Creeks had been staked. Henderson spent the rest of his life bitter and resentful of Carmack.

Joe Ladue, a trader, had a sawmill in Ogilvie, upriver from the big discovery. In September 1896, he moved his sawmill down to a swampy area on the Yukon River near the mouth of the Klondike River. He filed a claim and staked out a town site. He named the town Dawson. Ladue became extremely wealthy during the following year from selling off the lots in his new town.

There were no telephones or telegraphs to announce the discovery to the Outside. Prospectors from all parts of Alaska and the Yukon Territory heard about the discovery by word of mouth and came to stake their claims.

News of the gold strike reached Circle City, Alaska, in the late fall of 1896. It was 220 miles downstream from the Klondike.

It was common for rumors to spread about strikes. The sourdoughs were skeptical about chasing across the country only to find the rumor was not true. But in January 1897, a Circle City saloon keeper named Harry Ash received a letter from his partner in the Klondike. His partner had "hit it big." Ash tore off his apron and told the miners in his saloon that they could drink up his booze. He headed for the Klondike.

Soon most of the miners in Circle City had loaded their food, tents, and mining equipment onto dogsleds. By spring Circle City was almost a ghost town, and Dawson had become a tent city of about fifteen hundred people. By summer another thousand people were living in tents in Dawson.

By September 1897, 1,203 gold claims had been recorded in the Yukon District. The fee to record a claim was $15, which was good for one year. A miner could renew his claim every year for $100, but he had to work the claim for at least three months in a row sometime during the year.

The miners who made the early claims on the creeks were lucky. But some made unlucky decisions. Many miners doubted there really was gold. They either abandoned their claims or sold them cheap. Others couldn't afford to buy equipment to work their claims. Still others lost their claims in card games, for many of the miners were perpetual gamblers.

John Zarnowsky, known as Russian John, decided his claim number 30 on Bonanza Creek would not pay. He traded it to "Big Alex" McDonald for a side of bacon and a sack of flour. McDonald worked the claim and took out $5,000 in a single day.

McDonald bought interest in ten claims on Eldorado, seven on Bonanza, and about fifty more on other creeks. He also owned land in Dawson. He had so many holdings, he could hardly keep up with them. Often when meeting someone, he would ask, "Are you one of my partners?" It is believed Alex McDonald was worth almost $20 million at one time. He became known as the King of the Klondike.

Charley Anderson was called the Lucky Swede. While he was drunk, he paid $800 for claim number 29 on Eldorado. The next day he tried to get his money back. Of course, the sellers would not refund his money. Stuck with number 29, Anderson decided to work it. Within four years the claim yielded $1,250,000.

Dick Lowe, an ex–mule skinner, found an 86-foot fraction. A fraction was an unclaimed section lying between two other claims. Fractions were the result of mistakes made in measuring claims and in exceeding the legal 500-foot limit. Lowe claimed the fraction but then tried to sell it for $900. No one was interested. With nothing better to do that winter, Lowe worked the claim. Altogether he took out $500,000. That fraction of a claim proved to be the richest piece of land of its size the world has known. Dick Lowe squandered his fortune and died in 1907.

Thomas Lippy had left his job at the Seattle YMCA. He staked number 36 on Eldorado Creek. But Lippy's wife, who had come north with him, wanted a cabin. So Lippy abandoned his first claim and moved down the creek to number 16, which had been staked then abandoned by a group of men. Lippy staked number 16 because the timber was better for building a cabin. He made the right decision. There was little gold in the upper Eldorado, but Lippy took $1,530,000 from number 16.

Robert Henderson sold his Gold Bottom claim for $3,000. That claim eventually yielded more than $650,000 in gold.

Thomas Lippy packs out gold from his Eldorado Creek claim. He took out more than $1.5 million from his claims in the Klondike.

CHAPTER 5

---◆---

TONS OF GOLD

In the spring of 1897, the ice on the rivers finally broke up and steamboats could get through. When the first steamboats arrived in Dawson, more than eighty prospectors were waiting for passage south. For many of them, this would be their first trip home in several years.

They were going home with more than three tons of gold.

On July 15, 1897, the old rusty steamship *Excelsior* arrived in San Francisco. People stared as the dirty, weather-beaten miners came down the gangplank.

Thomas Lippy and his wife struggled with a bulging suitcase containing 200 pounds of gold. Fred Price, who had been a laundryman in Seattle, carried $15,000 in gold.

Miners carried the gold in bags, glass jars, packing cases, boxes, medicine bottles, tomato cans, and blankets tied with cords and straps. They hired a wagon to take them to Selby Smelting Works on Montgomery Street, since the United States Mint was closed for the day. It was estimated that a ton of gold was brought ashore that day.

Within hours of the *Excelsior*'s arrival in San Francisco, the ship's return voyage was sold out. Ten times the number of ticket purchasers had to be turned away.

By the next day the news had flashed across the country about a gold strike in the Canadian Yukon. Rumors circulated that the gold was lying in the streambeds waiting for people to "scoop it up." C. J. Berry, who was returning from the Klondike, was quoted in the San Francisco *Chronicle* as saying, "Two million dollars taken from the Klondyke region in less than five months, and a hundred times that amount awaiting those who can handle a pick and shovel. . . ."

The mayor of Seattle, W. D. Wood, happened to be in San Francisco at the time. When he heard about the gold discovery in the north, he sent a telegraph to the Seattle City Council resigning his post as mayor. He was going to the Yukon.

Beriah Brown, a reporter for *The Seattle Post-Intelligencer*, chartered a tugboat and went out to meet the steamship *Portland* when it entered Puget Sound. He wired a story back to Seattle and a special edition of the newspaper hit the streets just as the *Portland* was pulling in to Schwabacher's Dock.

The front page of *The Seattle Post-Intelligencer*, July 17, 1897

When the steamship *Portland* reached Schwabacher's Dock in Seattle at 6:00 A.M. on July 17, five thousand people were there to greet the passengers. As the miners came down the gangplank, the crowd shouted, "Hurrah for the Klondike!"

When Nils Anderson arrived on the dock, his wife was there to meet him. He had left two years earlier, having borrowed $300. His wife did not know he had struck it rich until he told her he had brought out over $100,000.

"Papa" William Stanley and his son had left Seattle in 1896 when he could not support his family as a bookseller. His wife took in laundry to keep her other children fed. When Stanley came down the gangplank of the *Portland*, he was carrying over $100,000 in gold dust. It is said his wife left her customers' wet clothes in the washtub and told them they could do their own laundry!

The city of Seattle went crazy. People stood in lines to try to buy tickets on a steamship going north. But the *Portland* had been sold out for her return voyage north before she had even reached the docks in Seattle.

CHAPTER 6

———◆———

CRAZINESS IN SEATTLE

Gold fever infected Seattle.

As the word spread, people all over the United States and the world joined the gold rush. They sold their belongings or borrowed from family and friends to get a grubstake. By July 18, 1897, two thousand New Yorkers had tried to buy tickets to the Klondike.

To be going to the Klondike was thrilling. Many wore buttons that read, "I'm going," or "I'm going this spring." The stampeder was a sort of hero, envied by those not going.

Once the stampeders arrived in Seattle, they put on their heavy woolen coats, new boots, wide-brimmed hats, and furs and had their pictures taken by photographers. A photograph was a great way to share this adventure with the folks back home. Klondike clothing also got the stampeder a free drink in any saloon.

Before the gold rush, a ticket from Seattle to Dawson cost $150; Seattle to Skagway or Dyea cost between $30 and $50. When thousands of people stood in line to buy passage, the price on the all-water route went up to $1,000. The stampeders paid extra to ship their food, equipment, and animals such as packhorses. Once in line, people would not give up their place to sleep or eat.

Dogs in Seattle mysteriously disappeared. Any dog that weighed more than forty pounds and had some strength was drafted for a career in pulling a dogsled—usually without the knowledge of the dog's owner.

And then there were the ideas and inventions.

The Klondike Combined Sledge and Boat Company offered a "sectional steel sledge-and-barge," with sails, oars, and air chambers so that it would float. It also had burglar-proof compartments for storing the gold. Potential buyers found it to be useless.

The Yukon Mining School opened in Seattle to teach prospectors how to prospect for gold.

"General" Jacob S. Coxey invented a vehicle that attached to a bicycle. The miner was to load part of his equipment and drag the vehicle about ten miles. He would then leave that portion of his outfit, fold up the side wheels, and ride the vehicle back as a bicycle to get another load. It was strange looking. And it didn't work.

C. L. "Barrel" Smith of Houston, Texas, built himself a vehicle to get to the Klondike. The axles ran through barrels instead of wheels. The barrels were loaded with one thousand pounds of supplies. He hitched a team of horses to the contraption, but everything fell apart before he got half a mile.

There were other "bright" ideas.

The Trans-Alaskan Gopher Company sold stock in its school, which planned to train arctic gophers to dig holes in the frozen ground and save miners the work.

Thomas Arnold tried to get investors for his Alaska Carrier Pigeon Mail Service. He intended to get the mail between Juneau and the goldfields. This idea also did not work.

Another inventor tried to sell a felt-lined portable cabin.

Another offered X-ray machines that could detect underground deposits of gold.

For a fee, clairvoyants, people who claim to perceive things that are not in sight, would tell stampeders where to look for gold. One woman's fee was $2,000.

And other contraptions were available: a gold crusher, a special Klondike bicycle that would scoop up pay dirt with little effort from the miner, Klondike protection hats, Klondike frost extractors, Klondike sectional boats, Klondike eyeglasses, Klondike medicine chests, Klondike soup, mechanical gold pans, collapsible boats, scurvy cures, and sleds powered by gasoline motors or by steam.

Business on Railroad Avenue in Seattle increased with the gold rush.

Three men planned to suck gold from the creeks using compressed air.

Many stampeders planned to bicycle to the Klondike.

These people were what the natives called cheechakos, which means "tenderfeet" or "newcomers." They were about to enter a fierce and rugged country with very little knowledge about how to survive.

CHAPTER 7

---◆---

GOLD FEVER

For some it was greed. For some it was adventure. For many it was their last hope.

People of all professions had gold fever.

In Seattle there were so many people in the streets that the streetcars couldn't get through. They would not have gotten through anyway: Half of the streetcar motormen had quit their jobs so that they could go to the Klondike.

Catholic nuns went. University football players went. The prizefighter Montana Kid went. So did farmers, clerks, cowboys, bakers, bankers, doctors, seamen, students, preachers, entertainers, lawyers, dentists, businessmen, and members of the Salvation Army.

Twelve of Seattle's police officers resigned within four days. Most of Tacoma's fire department resigned. Stores closed since their clerks had walked out—heading for the goldfields. Jurors in San Francisco threatened to quit if a trial was too long. They, too, wanted to leave for the goldfields!

The day after the *Portland's* arrival, the steamer *Al-ki* left Seattle. It is amazing that it was underway less than twenty-four hours after the gold rush began.

The *Al-ki* was the first gold rush steamer to leave Seattle. It was filled with 110 passengers, 350 tons of miners' supplies, 900 sheep, 65 cattle, and 50 horses. The ship was only 201 feet long.

By July 27, fifteen hundred people had left Seattle for the Klondike. Nine more ships were in the harbor, loaded and ready to sail.

During the middle week of August alone, 2,800 people sailed from Seattle for the Klondike. By the first of September, 9,000 people and 36,000 tons of equipment and supplies had left from Seattle.

Newspapers ran articles of advice, information, and news of good fortune. But there were also warnings coming out of the

Posters such as this were displayed in Seattle, advertising the various steamships going north.

North. Too many people were pouring in and there would not be enough food during the coming winter.

People in Dawson began to panic. Six steamboats carrying supplies were headed for Dawson, but they got stranded on sandbars when the river became too shallow to navigate. Captain John J. Healy felt certain *his* ship would arrive with food and supplies. He was partly right. His vessel came into port in Dawson before the freeze-up. But when it was unloaded, it was carrying only whiskey! Someone downriver had decided there was not enough profit in food and sent whiskey instead.

The residents of Dawson were warned they must leave. Many tried to get downriver, but the river froze and trapped the steamers in the ice before they could get to St. Michael. Some residents went through the mountains, but most of them lost fingers and toes to frostbite. Meanwhile, people from all over Canada, the United States, and the world were rushing to get to the Yukon for their share of the gold.

During the winter of 1897–98, a million people made plans to go to the Klondike. Approximately 100,000 stampeders actually started out. Forty thousand reached the Yukon goldfields by the summer of 1898. The rest either got a short distance and returned home or reached Seattle and discovered they could not afford to outfit themselves and pay for ship passage.

Most of the stampeders were men, but women also went to the Klondike. Many went with their husbands, but others went for the adventure. Some wives set out while their husbands stayed home. Some women went to support their families. Some caught gold fever and went strictly for the riches. Some went as newspaper reporters.

Most of the people who set out for the Klondike had led sedentary lives and were not in condition for the difficult trip that lay ahead of them. They were not in physical shape to get a ton of supplies two thousand miles north. They knew little about packing, pack animals, tenting, wilderness survival, enduring arctic weather, building boats, or navigation.

Most hardly knew where the Yukon or the Klondike was.

Some trusted experts to give them advice, but often those "experts" were giving advice strictly for their own profit.

The majority of the men who headed for the Klondike had only a vague idea of the hardships they were about to face. They believed they would pick gold nuggets out of a stream with little effort, and some even took sacks along in which to carry home the gold. Each was convinced he would return a wealthy man.

CHAPTER 8

—◆◆◆—

WHAT THEY TOOK

When the gold rush started on Bonanza Creek, the North-West Mounted Police could see there would be trouble if law and order weren't established. They sent eighty officers to the region, investing $400,000 in law enforcement.

Further, the trading posts couldn't get enough food for all the people. The North-West Mounted Police issued an order requiring each stampeder to bring three pounds of food per day for a year. They would not let anyone cross the border into Canada unless they had packed the required food. The list of necessary supplies was provided to stampeders before they even left Seattle.

The most widely distributed list was made up by the Northern Pacific Railroad, which brought most of the stampeders west to Seattle, but there were other lists as well.

FOOD

- bacon, 200 pounds
- flour, 400 pounds
- assorted dried fruit, 85 pounds (*apples, peaches, apricots, plums*)
- cornmeal, 50 pounds
- rice, 35 pounds
- coffee, 24 pounds
- tea, 5 pounds
- sugar, 100 pounds
- fish, 25 pounds

- soup vegetables, 15 pounds
- oatmeal, 50 pounds
- dried potatoes, 50 pounds
- dried onions, 50 pounds
- butter, 25 cans
- beans, 100 pounds
- condensed milk, 4 dozen tins
- salt, 15 pounds
- pepper, 1 pound
- baking powder, 8 pounds
- baking soda, 2 pounds
- mustard, ½ pound
- ginger, ¾ pound
- yeast cakes, 36 pounds
- matches, 60 boxes
- soap, 5 bars

CLOTHING

- 1 suit oil clothing
- 3 pairs snag-proof rubber boots
- 3 pairs heavy shoes
- 1 dozen heavy socks
- 6 pairs woolen mittens
- 3 suits heavy underwear
- 2 pairs mackinaw trousers
- 2 pairs overalls
- 2 hats
- 4 heavy woolen overshirts
- 1 heavy mackinaw coat
- 1 heavy rubber-lined coat
- suspenders, handerkerchiefs, snow glasses
- 2 pairs of heavy woolen blankets
- 2 oil blankets
- 4 towels
- buttons, thread, needles
- 5 yards mosquito netting

EQUIPMENT

- 1 large bucket
- 1 set granite buckets
- 2 axes, plus extra handle
- 2 picks
- handsaw
- whipsaw
- 1 shovel
- pack strap
- 6 files
- drawing knife
- brace and bits
- jack plane
- hammer
- 3 chisels
- butcher knife
- ⅜-inch rope, 200 feet
- pitch, 10 pounds
- oakum, 5 pounds
- 2 caulking irons
- nails, 15 pounds
- tent
- canvas
- whet stone
- compass
- goggles
- quartz glass
- quicksilver
- 2 frying pans
- coffee and tea pot
- candles, 40 pounds
- eating utensils: plate, cup, knife, fork, spoon
- pots and pans
- steel stove for 4 men
- gold pan
- gold scales

Also, medicines, reading matter, guns, ammunition, and personal items were suggested. Some miners chose to take along a Yukon sled.

One Seattle newspaper estimated the cost of the outfit would be $140. Another estimated $500. Seattle outfitters, businesses that sold the supplies to the stampeders, estimated the total would be around $1,000. If this doesn't sound like much money, remember that in 1897 a person could buy a meal in a good restaurant for 25 cents.

"Steerers" met the trains bringing people into Seattle from all over the United States. Working for the outfitters, they mingled with the crowds and guided customers to their outfitter's store so that the stampeders would not buy from a competitor.

It was extremely difficult for a man to travel alone, so many stampeders formed partnerships. It made sense to share equipment such as stoves, buckets, axes, and cooking pans. A partnership meant less to purchase and less for each man to carry. On the trail, partners could take turns standing guard at one cache of equipment while the others packed up the trail.

Businesses called outfitters sold everything a stampeder would need for his trip to the Klondike. Outfitters in Seattle stayed open day and night.

The Seattle horse markets did a big business. Animals sold easily—broncos, swaybacked nags, mules, and oxen from logging camps. Skinny, worn-out old horses were brought in from Montana, where they were bought for $3 to $5. In Seattle, they were sold to stampeders for $25 and up. Goats, sheep, ponies, burros, mules, oxen, dogs, and reindeer were also sold as pack animals.

The list of a year's supplies seems overwhelming. Yet some people also took merchandise to start businesses in Dawson or to sell along the trail.

Some went as tourists, such as Miss Blanche King. At forty-seven years old, she bought passage on the all-water route and took along a horse, a parrot, three canaries, a piano, two Saint Bernards, a maid, a cook, and a sealskin suit.

As each ship—loaded beyond its capacity—left the harbor, crowds on the dock cheered, "Hurrah for the Klondike!" It was almost as if soldiers were leaving for a war—a war each man expected to win.

CHAPTER 9

———◆———

THE JOURNEY BEGINS

All the West Coast port cities tried to get the stampeders to outfit in their city—Vancouver and Victoria, British Columbia; San Francisco, California; Portland, Oregon; and Tacoma, Washington. But Seattle's chamber of commerce advertised all over the nation and even overseas. Calling itself the Gateway to the Goldfields, its advertising paid off. Thousands of people flocked to Seattle. The Klondike gold rush poured $25 million into Seattle by the spring of 1898. Only $5 million altogether went to other cities.

Seattle even had jobs for those *not* going to the goldfields!

THE ALL-WATER ROUTE

The all-water route, or "the rich man's route," was the safest way to the Klondike and required the least amount of work. It was estimated to be 2,750 miles by ocean steamer from Seattle to St. Michael, where the Yukon River empties into the Bering Sea. The passengers then transferred to river steamers and traveled 1,700 miles up the Yukon to Dawson.

It could be a six-week trip in excellent weather. But the steamboats could get up the Yukon River only during two to three months of the year, and then they made frequent stops. Even in good weather, boilers blew up or the boats hit sandbars, mudflats, and sunken snags. Once the river froze, the boats couldn't move until the spring thaw, when the ice broke up.

Eighteen hundred stampeders left for St. Michael in the summer of 1897. Forty-three reached Dawson in 1897 before the winter freeze-up. The rest were stranded at various points along the Yukon River, their ships frozen in the ice. The frustrated passengers sat idly for eight months with nothing to do. They imagined other stampeders were already scooping up the gold.

One well-known group that got stranded in the ice had been organized by W. D. Wood, who had resigned as mayor of Seattle when the *Excelsior* had arrived in San Francisco loaded with gold. Wood's ship was ready to leave port a month later, but there was trouble. Wood had overloaded the vessel and was attempting to leave behind 50,000 pounds of gear belonging to the people who had joined his party. They threatened to lynch him right there on the dock. The matter was resolved and the gear was loaded.

When the ship arrived in St. Michael, the party learned they would have to construct their own riverboat. That was not what they had planned, but they built the boat. By the time they left St. Michael, they were still 1,700 miles from Dawson. Soon after, the Yukon winter set in. The river froze and the party was stranded. They went ashore and built a makeshift settlement, which they called Suckersville.

The group was so unhappy with Wood that he set out on foot back to St. Michael. The rest of the group survived the winter and in the spring went on to Dawson. Most of them immediately turned around and went home. The only good part of the trip was that no one lost his life.

A SHORTAGE OF SHIPS

Because so many people wanted passage north, more ships were needed to carry the miners and their equipment. Most stampeders had to go at least partway by boat.

Before the gold rush, seven ships ran between Seattle and Alaska on a regular schedule. When thousands of people lined up to buy tickets for the trip north, every boat was put into service—old side-wheel steamers, barges, coalers, yachts, sloops, and even condemned sailing schooners. Vessels once deemed

The steamship *Australia* prepares to leave Seattle for the Klondike.

unseaworthy were being pulled from ship graveyards. After some quick repairs, they were sent to the North.

Unfortunately many of the ships were not safe. They lost power. The steering went out. Crews were often inexperienced, and some captains had never before navigated through Alaskan waters. Ships ran aground. They hit rocks, took on water, and sank. In 1898 an average of three ships wrecked each month.

Besides being unseaworthy, most ships provided deplorable living conditions. They were overloaded. Every inch of space above and below decks was filled with people, their food, their gear, animals, and general cargo.

Steamship companies often sold the same berth or cabin to more than one person. Fights would break out between passengers or between passengers and the crew.

One ship built to carry one hundred passengers was booked for five hundred. People were assigned ten to a cabin. Whenever a person left a bunk, someone else got in. The ship's dining area could seat only twenty-six people, so meals were served in shifts.

Stowaways, people on board who had not paid their fare, were common. So many people were on board that no one could tell the passengers who had paid from those who had not.

On one ship, horses were wedged so tightly together that they could not lie down. They rode beside the engines, and when the engines throbbed or the whistle blew, the terrified horses reared, kicked, and bit the animals next to them.

Safety was not a priority. Bales of hay to feed horses were piled on deck, blocking the view from the ship's bridge. Howling and yapping dogs in pens were also stacked on the decks.

One ship, the *Clara Nevada,* was illegally carrying passengers and dynamite. It blew up before it reached Skagway, killing all sixty-five passengers and crew members. One dog survived.

The food was terrible. Comfort and cleanliness were secondary concerns. The important thing was to get to the northlands any way possible. At the ticket office, the stampeders didn't care how many people were already on the boat. They just wanted passage. But once the trip began, the passengers were miserable.

Those who rode belowdecks were sickened by the smell. On many ships the animals were transported belowdecks and there was no one to remove the manure. On other ships the animals rode on deck, but their excretions leaked between the deck's floorboards onto the people sleeping in berths below. Many of the people who rode below suffered from seasickness. Their vomit together with the animal manure made the stench almost unbearable.

Further, there was no way for the passengers to stay clean. People slept in their clothes and the body odor was terrible. Some people preferred riding on deck in the rain or bitter cold and risking pneumonia to riding belowdecks.

Living conditions on the boats were bad, but the worst was yet to come.

CHAPTER 10

———◆•◆———

THE INSIDE
PASSAGE ROUTES

Most of the stampeders chose to go partway by ship and the rest of the way overland. They traveled by boat to either Dyea or Skagway through the inside passage. Under ideal conditions, the trip took about six to eight days. Unfortunately the conditions were seldom ideal.

Many of those with packhorses chose to disembark at Skagway and hike over White Pass.

When the first stampeders arrived in Skagway on July 26, 1897, the summer rains had created mud that came to the knees of both men and horses. Blankets were wet at night. Stampeders tried to dry their wet hats and socks by the fire, but the damp wood only smoked and smoldered. Everyone was muddy and wet and tired.

Skagway or Dyea was as far as some of the men got. Realizing the enormous journey ahead of them, a few opened a temporary restaurant and sold the beans and bacon they had brought north. With the small profit, they paid for a return ticket home.

As if the stampeders didn't have enough problems, a thirty-seven-year-old swindler settled in Skagway in 1897. Jefferson

Randolph "Soapy" Smith brought with him a gang of thugs, gamblers, shell-game operators, and dance-hall girls. His criminals ran a saloon, crooked gambling halls, a merchant's exchange, a discount ticket office, and an information office.

The "Reverend" Charles Bowers was a phony minister. He gained the stampeders' trust as soon as they got into town. Billy Saportas claimed to be a newspaper reporter. He interviewed the newcomers to see how much money they had. Slim Jim Foster helped carry people's loads into town from the dock. He either led them to Soapy's saloon or referred them to phony packers. The packers never hauled a thing—just stole the miners' equipment. Old Man Tripp pretended to be an old sourdough. He gave newcomers "valuable information" and referred them to other members of the gang, such as Yank Fewclothes, King of Terrors, Jay Bird Slim, Fatty Green, or Kid Jimmy Fresh.

Soapy Smith (fourth man from the right) and some of his gang members.

Soapy ran a telegraph company that had no telegraph equipment. Telegraph lines had not yet reached Alaska in 1897, but Soapy's telegraph office would send miners' messages for five dollars. He even got phony responses—collect, which meant the miner had to pay to receive the response.

After a stampeder had lost his entire outfit and all his money, Soapy himself would appear. Hearing the miner's story, he would give the victim some money—in the name of Christian charity. It would be just enough money to buy passage back to Seattle. The victims always left town without creating a scene, grateful for the generosity of Jefferson Randolph "Soapy" Smith.

Sam Steele of the Canadian North-West Mounted Police called Skagway "the roughest place in the world." But Steele had no jurisdiction there since it was part of Alaska and under the jurisdiction of the United States. There were murders and robberies every day, but the U.S. marshal assigned to Skagway worked for Soapy Smith.

Soapy Smith was finally killed on July 8, 1898, by a man named Frank Reid in a shoot-out over the theft of gold from another miner. Soapy's gang of criminals either left town or were prosecuted.

For those who managed to avoid the criminals in Skagway, the White Pass was the next treacherous part of their journey. Those who disembarked in Dyea went over the Chilkoot Pass. Either route took the stampeders to Lake Lindeman or Lake Bennett. There they built boats for the 550-mile river journey to Dawson and the Klondike goldfields.

THE WHITE PASS

The difficulties of crossing White or Chilkoot Pass were unbelievable. The White Pass trail was not as steep a climb as the Chilkoot Pass trail. For those who brought animals or could afford to hire a professional pack train, White Pass seemed to be an easier and quicker trail.

The 45-mile trail over White Pass began easily with a wagon road that followed the Skagway River.

But the White Pass trail was a series of loose gravel, marshes and muskeg, shallow streams, and boulders and included about a mile of sand. The trail along a sheer granite cliff called Devil's Hill was barely two feet wide in places. There were drop-offs where a misstep could mean a 500-foot fall to death. Porcupine Hill was strewn with 10-foot boulders. Summit Hill was a 1,000-foot climb through knee-deep mud holes and rocks that ripped the horses' feet and bodies.

Those who crossed White Pass without a pack animal carried their loads along five-mile intervals, 65 pounds at a time. At the end of each stretch, they would start a cache. They would return with another load, again . . . and again . . . and again. . . . Some men walked 2,500 miles to move their outfits to Lake Bennett—30 round trips.

Moving a ton of food and equipment over White Pass was exhausting. This stampeder fell asleep on the trail.

A few brought large sleds called sledges to move their goods. Even with a sledge, it took a stampeder at least 90 days to move everything over the 45 miles.

This lunch break might look like a picnic, but these stampeders had a long journey yet ahead of them.

The men along the trail gasped and groaned under the weight of their loads. Bent almost double, they staggered forward in a human chain that went unbroken for hours.

There were reports one woman strapped bread dough to her back. As she climbed, the heat of her body cooked the dough into bread, which she sold at the end of the day!

A. J. Goddard and his wife moved two stern-wheel steamboats over the summit—piece by piece.

A group of partners herded 100 turkeys over White Pass. It was summer, so the turkeys had plenty of berries to eat on the trail. At night the turkeys roosted in the treetops.

Eric A. Hegg was a well-known photographer of the Klondike. He used a team of long-haired goats to pull a sledge carrying his photographic equipment.

In August 1897, after a six-day storm of freezing rain on White Pass, some stampeders got separated from their partners. They were soaked and had no food, no tent, no coffee. Other stampeders sipped hot coffee or slept in their tents just a few feet away but would not offer hospitality. Their excuse? "We worked hard to get here and we don't want to be crowded."

Not everyone was cruel. A twenty-four-year-old Irish woman, Mollie Walsh, opened a grub tent on the other side of the White Pass summit. She fed many hungry prospectors. Kind and friendly, she won the heart of everyone she met.

Two professional packers fell in love with Mollie. "Packer Jack" Newman wanted to marry her, but she married Mike Bartlett instead. Mollie and Mike Bartlett moved to Seattle; he

Mollie Walsh won the hearts of many on the White Pass trail.

"Packer Jack" Newman prepares to leave Skagway for Lake Bennett. He fell in love with Mollie Walsh after she took care of his frozen hand in a blizzard.

killed her in 1902. Newman never forgot Mollie. Years later he had a monument erected in Skagway in her memory.

Only about half of those who started over the White Pass trail actually moved all their gear to Lake Bennett. Some turned back. Some got ill from food poisoning, grippe, pneumonia, or meningitis.

The worst tragedy of the White Pass trail was the animals. Thousands of horses had been shipped north to pack supplies. Most of them were not appropriate for this kind of work. Some were wild. Some were old. But White Pass was a death trap even for animals suited for packing. The narrow trail twisted and turned, and horses fell to their deaths in the valley below.

Forced to wade through mud to their bellies, the animals slipped, flailed in sinkholes, and drowned. Seventeen horses went down in one place. It would take hours for an owner to pull one horse out of the mud. The trail was too narrow for anyone to go around, so other stampeders and animals would have to wait. They might have to stand with packs on their backs for twenty-four hours before they could move forward.

Many of the problems were caused by inexperienced packers. Some of the men had had desk or counter jobs before joining the gold rush. They had never learned how to load a pack on an animal. When a horse wasn't packed correctly, loads tore sores in the animal's hide. Some of the horses died from fevers brought on by infected wounds. Their hooves were injured by the sharp rocks. Injuries were neither treated nor allowed to heal. Some stampeders, eager to stake their claim for gold, would beat their animals unmercifully.

When the animals died on the trail, the stampeders left the carcasses where they lay. Other stampeders walked over or around the bodies. The trail, littered with the bodies of three thousand dead animals, became impassable. It was called the Dead Horse Trail.

Jack London, who later became a famous writer, was one of the first Klondikers to cross the mountains. In one of his short stories, he wrote about the Dead Horse Trail: "Their hearts turned to stone—those which did not break—and they became beasts, the men on Dead Horse Trail."

Many of the animals that actually got over the pass to Lake Bennett were then turned loose, since the owners had no fur-

Many horses died on the White Pass trail. When the spring rains created floods, the bodies of the horses floated downriver. In this photo the bodies of horses are decaying in the Skagway River outside of Skagway. The smell was terrible.

ther need for them. There was not enough vegetation for them to feed on, so most of those animals starved to death.

The professional packers took good care of their animals. The animals were, after all, making them money. They would carry enough feed for the animals, blanket them at night, and even warm water for the animals to drink. They also packed the loads on the animals correctly so that the boxes would not gouge their hides or throw the animals off balance, causing them to fall.

Joe Brooks arrived in Skagway with 17 mules. He bought more mules and soon had 335. He often made $5,000 a day packing.

Mrs. Harriet Pullen was a packer on White Pass. Her husband had died and she was raising four children. When she first arrived in Skagway, she baked pies and sold them for one dollar each. Once she had enough money, she got into the packing business. Mrs. Pullen remained in Skagway the rest of her life.

THE CHILKOOT PASS

The thirty-three-mile Chilkoot Pass trail was more heavily used than the White Pass trail. While it was stormier, steeper, and more slippery (from rain in the summer and fall, from snow and ice in the spring and winter), it was still the best route.

Passengers coming north by steamship disembarked at Dyea, about nine miles from Skagway. The water was not deep enough for the boat to get close to the shore and there was no wharf. Horses were suspended over the side of the ship and dropped into the water to swim ashore. Passengers and their supplies were loaded onto rafts, scows, or barges to

A family starts out on the Chilkoot Pass trail with a native boy working as a packer.

A scow brings a load of stampeders and their outfits from the steamship to the shores near Dyea.

be taken ashore and unloaded. Then everything had to be moved to higher ground, as the tide would come in quickly and the water would rise as much as thirty feet.

Sometimes the stampeder could not work fast enough. The tide would come in and soak everything—flour, sugar, dried milk, coffee, tea, oatmeal, salt, baking soda, dried potatoes. Grown men would sink to their knees, sobbing. They had lost the outfit in which they had invested their life's savings a few weeks earlier.

In some cases when the gear was taken ashore by scow or barge, it was stacked in giant heaps. Each stampeder had to scramble to find his belongings.

From Dyea the stampeders carried their outfits to Canyon City. There a pack train of ten horses could be hired for $100 per day. Or a wagon and team could be hired for $25 per day. Many native men, women, and children hired out as packers. The natives charged 5¢ per pound at the beginning of the rush. The price went up to 10¢, then 17¢, then 30¢, then 40¢ per pound. They raised their prices every week! Few stampeders could afford to hire packers.

The next settlement was Pleasant Camp, then Sheep Camp. Sheep Camp was the last point where the stampeder could cut firewood. At Sheep Camp, a stampeder could get a meal of bacon, beans, and tea for $2.50—about the price of two days' wages. The Palmer Hotel, a 20-foot by 40-foot one-room cabin, was run by a husband and wife and their seven children. They served 500 meals a day, and charged seventy-five cents each, payable in advance. At night forty stampeders hung their wet shoes and socks on the rafters and slept on the floor. "Guests" were packed in so tightly one against the next that no one could enter or leave during the night.

Beyond Sheep Camp they struggled to Stone House, which was a giant boulder where the stampeders could stop to rest.

Stampeders and a native packer rest along a rocky portion of the Chilkoot Pass trail near Stone House.

The next stopping place was the Scales. Packers charged by the pound to carry gear, so gear was weighed at the Scales. Packers charged a dollar per pound for this leg of the trip.

After the Scales, it was three miles to the summit. But it was a very steep three miles—the trail had a 35-degree incline.

The weather was terrible on Chilkoot Pass. Some days the wind blew so hard that travelers couldn't stand upright. White-outs were common. There were days when the stampeders were forced to stay in tents or crude shelters to escape the rain or snow. Sometimes the stampeders crawled up the icy slopes on their hands and knees.

Stampeders use a ladder to move their supplies over a frozen waterfall on the difficult Chilkoot Pass trail.

In February 1898, approximately fifteen hundred steps, called the Golden Stairs, were carved into the ice along the steepest part of the climb. A rope was strung along the side of the stairs so the stampeders wouldn't lose their balance. They each carried at least fifty pounds of supplies on their backs. Benches were also carved so that a stampeder could step out of line to rest.

Climbing the Golden Stairs to the summit took most men six hours. And they didn't do it just once. They went back for another load . . . and another . . . and another. . . .

With so many fierce storms, it took most men three months to get all their gear moved. One stampeder wrote that he and his partners hiked nearly one thousand miles back and forth on the Chilkoot Trail, moving their goods the thirty-three miles to Lake Bennett.

Having at least two partners—and it was better to have three—was especially helpful in reaching the summit. One could guard the supplies at one end of the trail. The others could pack up the trail. The partner left behind could also cook.

Going back down the mountain for another load was easy. Some used their shovels or gold pans as sleds. Others just slid down.

The first tramway to the summit of Chilkoot Pass began running in December 1897. Five were in operation by the following May. Trams cost between 5¢ and 35¢ per pound, depending on the season and the type of load to be transported. That was more than most stampeders could afford.

At the summit of Chilkoot Pass the stampeders stacked their supplies and marked their caches with shovels. Snowstorms were fierce on top of the pass. Four to five feet of snow would

Most stampeders made the strenuous climb up the Golden Stairs to Chilkoot Pass at least forty times. Coming down from the summit, the speed was terrific. The trail down was called the grease trail.

fall in a few hours, and temperatures would drop to fifty degrees below zero. A stampeder traveling alone or with just one partner often returned to his cache on top of the mountain to find it buried. Seventy feet of snow fell on the summit of Chilkoot Pass that winter, and some men couldn't find their outfits until the spring thaw.

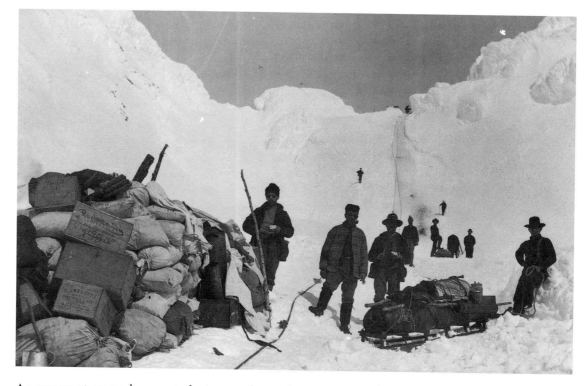

As more stampeders got their goods to the summit of Chilkoot Pass, the stacks of supplies began to resemble buildings in a strange city.

The summit of Chilkoot Pass began to resemble a small city with narrow passages for streets. Instead of houses, there were stacks of supplies.

At the summit, Canadian customs and immigration officers collected duties on all goods taken into Canada. They worked out of a small tent flying the British flag. Stampeders had to pay 20 to 35 percent of each item's value in customs. Each stampeder also had to prove he had enough supplies to last a year.

Besides collecting the tax, the officials also gathered information about each stampeder. The stampeders had to register at regular posts along the route to Dawson. If someone failed to report at the next registration point, the North-West Mounted

Police would investigate. This procedure was to provide help in case there was an accident, and it was a way of catching criminals.

In the spring, avalanches were common. In an avalanche on April 3, 1898, thousands of tons of wet snow covered everything in its path. The native packers had warned the stampeders that they should avoid the mountain that day. Some stampeders heeded the advice, but everyone had been halted for two weeks by bad weather and they were eager to make progress. Over seventy people were buried alive.

Within twenty minutes of the avalanche, the men from Sheep Camp began digging out bodies. They found between six and ten survivors—and more than sixty lifeless bodies.

According to the *Seattle Post-Intelligencer,* not every event on Chilkoot Pass was tragic. A week before the avalanche—March 1898—there was a wedding. Maria Isharov, a twenty-year-old Pole, had met thirty-year-old Frank Brady, a miner from Montana, on the trail. Frank and Maria fell in love and decided to get married. The wedding party proceeded up Chilkoot Pass as Phil Ward played his accordion. When the couple reached the summit, the Reverend Christopher L. Mortimer, a minister from Missouri, performed the ceremony.

People brought some very unusual items over Chilkoot Pass: pianos, glassware, crates of silk fabric, stuffed turkeys, a sack of old newspapers, a grindstone. A man from Iowa even brought his 125-pound plow.

Billy Huson and his wife packed a piano over Chilkoot Pass in the fall of 1897. They took the piano apart and wrapped the soundboard in wool yarn. Once they arrived in Dawson, Mrs. Huson knitted the yarn into sweaters and sold them. The piano sold to the Northern Saloon for $1,200.

One woman paid her way by giving banjo concerts on the trail.

The stampeders paid Arizona Charlie Meadows cash to watch him shoot the spots off a playing card at thirty feet.

A former railroad brakeman named Rugg had fallen under a railroad car thirteen years earlier and lost his left leg. With the support of his wooden leg, he relayed his gear in a sixty-pound pack on his back. Once he stopped for a few days and worked as a cook. Another time he worked piloting a ferry across the river. With his earnings of fifty dollars, he hired a packer to help him get his gear the rest of the way to Lake Lindeman.

Besides the hardships of the climb, there were many problems that faced the stampeders. An outbreak of spinal meningitis killed several dozen; seventeen people died in one night. Other dangers included food poisoning; pneumonia; respiratory ailments; accidents with guns, knives, and axes; and falls.

By the spring of 1898, 22,000 prospectors had passed over the summit of Chilkoot Pass. Over 60,000 people passed the summit in two years' time.

Those stampeders who actually crossed either White Pass or Chilkoot Pass felt triumphant. They had battled the trail and succeeded. They had faced the worst of weather conditions. They had escaped or survived illness. They had proved themselves physically fit to actually move two thousand pounds of supplies and equipment over the pass.

They could rightfully feel triumphant.

But an equal challenge still faced them.

THE REST OF THE WAY BY BOAT

Once the stampeders reached the summit of White or Chilkoot Pass, the hike to Lake Lindeman and Lake Bennett was somewhat easier. Those who crossed in the winter put their goods on sleds, made sails, and let the wind push them across frozen Crater Lake.

Once the stampeders reached frozen Crater Lake, they let the wind move their outfits across the ice. Crater Lake is a small lake—about two miles long—just over the summit of Chilkoot Pass on the way to Lake Lindeman or Lake Bennett.

From Lake Bennett, the remaining route was a water route, so the stampeders built boats to get to Dawson. Here it was particularly helpful to have at least one partner to share the work of building and navigating the boat.

By the end of the winter, the area around Lakes Lindeman and Bennett became the largest tent city in the world, home to some 30,000 people. The most common sounds in the huge tent city were of axes and saws as men chopped down trees. The trees had to be sawed into boards to make boats. Stampeders destroyed an entire forest in just a few months.

The North-West Mounted Police moved among the boatbuilders, offering advice and warning not to make "floating coffins." They assigned each boat a number and kept a record of its occupants.

The ice broke on May 29, 1898. Within forty-eight hours, 7,124 boats departed for the 550-mile waterway trip to Dawson. The outriggers, canoes, skiffs, kayaks, junks, scows, sidewheelers, arks, catamarans, catboats, dories, rowboats, and rafts carried about 30,000 people and 30 million pounds of food.

At Miles Canyon the canyon narrowed to about one hundred feet where the water flowed between high rock walls. The water was extremely deep and swift, with a maze of whirlpools and backwashes.

Two miles beyond Miles Canyon was a treacherous group

of white-water rapids called White Horse Rapids. Hundreds of outfits were lost in the rapids and whirlpools.

After 150 boats were wrecked and ten people drowned, the North-West Mounted Police regulated who could go through the rapids. Women and children were required to walk the five-mile trail. The Mounted Police required some stampeders to lower their boats through the rapids with ropes and carry their supplies around. They required other outfits to hire professional river pilots, who charged twenty-five dollars and up, to take the boats through the rapids.

In June Norman Macauley built a tram around Miles Canyon and White Horse Rapids. He laid tracks made of wooden poles and built flatbeds that were drawn by horses. His tram system carried tons of supplies around the dangerous water for three to five cents a pound.

Stampeders were required to register at each of the checkpoints. The police kept careful records of who had passed. If an outfit "forgot" to check in, a shot was fired across the bow of its boat as a reminder.

White Horse Rapids was the most dangerous part of the Yukon River journey. Crosses on the banks marked where stampeders lost their lives in the perilous waters.

CHAPTER 11

---◆---

THE OVERLAND ROUTES

There were several overland routes to the Yukon, but they were tragic and deadly.

THE BACK DOOR ROUTE

The "back door" route originated at Edmonton, Alberta, in Canada. It was advertised by Edmonton merchants and seemed like a wise choice for the stampeders who came from the East Coast and Europe, but it was anything but wise.

The map made the trip appear simple: Take a train to Edmonton and follow a well-marked trail to the Yukon. But there was no trail. The stampeders faced muskegs, willow thickets, flooding rivers, ravines that could not be crossed, and spruce forests so thick that many got lost.

About 1,500 men and 21 women left Edmonton in the fall of 1897, bound for the Yukon. At least 150 turned back before finishing even 100 miles of the trail. Between 5 and 30 people made it to Dawson by the end of 1898. Between 30 and 200 arrived by 1899. There were 70 recorded deaths, but it is estimated at least 500 died on the trail. A few prospected in the Canadian wilderness before reaching the Klondike. A few homesteaded in the Canadian wilderness. The rest turned back.

No one who took this route found any gold.

THE ROUTE THROUGH VALDEZ

An "all-American" route through Valdez, Alaska, seemed attractive, since Americans would avoid paying Canadian customs.

Of the 3,000 to 4,000 who began the journey at Valdez, only 200 successfully crossed Valdez Glacier and navigated the 25 miles of rapids of the Klutina River.

It is estimated that 15 to 20 people made it all the way to Dawson over this route. The rest did not have proper wilderness equipment, and most did not have pack animals. Many fell into crevasses in the glacier, were buried by avalanches, or drowned. Boats were smashed in the rivers. The weather was terrible.

People suffered painful snow blindness on the glacier. It was estimated that 70 percent of the miners who took this route suffered from mental derangement, babbling about a glacial demon. Almost everyone on this trail suffered some kind of physical suffering—scurvy, frostbite, starvation, or death by freezing.

When U.S. Army Captain William Ralph Abercrombie arrived in Valdez in the spring of 1898, he organized a rescue expedition. He and his team brought back approximately five hundred people who had spent the winter on the trail.

No one who took the Valdez route returned home with even a penny's worth of gold from the Klondike.

THE STIKINE, ASHCROFT, AND DALTON TRAILS

The Stikine route began at Wrangell, Alaska. Stampeders arrived in Wrangell by boat from the West Coast cities.

The Ashcroft trail began in Ashcroft, B.C. It was called the Poor Man's Route or the Long Trail. Ashcroft was only 125 miles northeast of Vancouver, B.C.

The two trails merged in Telegraph Creek or Glenora, B.C. They were popular with Canadians who wanted to avoid paying a U.S. duty on their outfits.

But these routes were treacherous. In the winter the Stikine River froze—but not solid. The icy slush made walking difficult. The trail also crossed swamps and river gorges.

Stampeders carried their outfits on their backs, pushed or pulled carts or wheelbarrows, or packed their belongings on animals. Three thousand pack animals, mostly horses, started this trail. But they fell over logs and rocks, slipped on the ice and snow, or drowned in mud holes. None of the animals reached Dawson. There were almost as many dead animals on this trail as there were on the Dead Horse Trail on White Pass. There just weren't as many stampeders along the Stikine route to tell of the conditions or to take photographs.

Of the 6,500 people who took these trails, only 200 to 300 actually reached Dawson. At least half of the stampeders turned back. Many died by drowning, disease, or from the terrible weather conditions. Murder and suicide were common.

DALTON TRAIL

Another route to the Yukon River was over a trail established by a colorful man named Jack Dalton. He charged a $250 toll to anyone using it.

The 300-mile route from Pyramid Harbor to old Fort Selkirk went through the mountains. It was hazardous but still better than some routes. From Fort Selkirk to Dawson on the Yukon River was another 175 miles.

Because it was 300 miles overland, the Dalton Trail took longer than the routes out of Skagway and Dyea, but it was more suitable for pack animals and cattle. In the summer of 1898, Jack Dalton became a "hero" in Dawson for bringing 2,000 beef cattle over his trail to Dawson, where there was a shortage of meat.

CHAPTER 12

———◆———

ARRIVING IN DAWSON

Eventually, whether they had come via water, over mountain passes, or through dense wilderness, thousands of stampeders made it to Dawson.

ARRIVING IN 1897

Some gold seekers arrived in the early spring of 1897. These were people who had already been living in the northlands—many in Circle City—and who had heard about the strike by word of mouth. That spring, there were still some claims to be staked. Other claims could be purchased at a reasonable cost.

By June 1897, Dawson's population was more than 4,000. There were jobs available. Miners often hired laborers to help work their claims.

Then prices began rising, the creeks were all staked, and the jobs were filled.

The sourdoughs knew that gold was found in the riverbeds, and all those claims had been staked. Then some cheechakos began staking claims on the hillsides. The sourdoughs laughed at their stupidity.

The sourdoughs didn't realize that some of the riverbeds had been lifted with the earth's movements millions of years before. When the cheechakos found these ancient riverbeds on the hillsides, they made fortunes.

It took more work to find the gold in the hillside claims. The shafts had to be dug deeper before reaching bedrock. Albert Lancaster dug 79 feet to reach bedrock in his claim on Gold Hill. But during the next eight weeks, he brought out an average of $2,000 worth of gold a day. The miner who staked next to Lancaster took out 30 pounds of gold in the first three days after he hit bedrock. Gold was selling for $17 an ounce at that time.

By the summer of 1897, Dawson's population had grown to 5,000. That was when the Outside was just getting the news of Carmack's big discovery. A few stampeders reached Dawson in the fall of 1897.

ARRIVING IN 1898

Most of the stampeders arrived in Dawson in late June or early July of 1898. These people had heard of Carmack's strike when the steamships *Excelsior* and *Portland* arrived in San Francisco and Seattle in July 1897.

The miners who had spent the winter in Dawson had few provisions. One stampeder brought eggs with him! He sold them for $18 a dozen.

One of the first men to arrive, Gene Allen, started a newspaper called the *Klondike Nugget*.

Twenty-two thousand people arrived in Dawson during the last week of June and the first week of July 1898. Most had come over Chilkoot or White Pass, but some had come up the river by steamer.

One stampeder brought a load of cats. He sold them for an ounce of gold apiece to miners who wanted the cats for company. One man arrived with candy, fresh fruits, and vegetables. These were luxuries in Dawson, and his apples sold for $1 each. His watermelons sold for $25 each. H. L. Miller brought a cow. The milk from that first cow sold for $30 a gallon.

When the stampeders arrived in Dawson, the town was clogged with more than 30,000 people, and city lots were selling for $20,000 each. There was almost no land available in town for pitching a tent or building a cabin. Buildings were half finished and streets were knee-deep in mud.

Once the stampeders arrived in Dawson, the "rush" was over. They had plenty of time to sit and decide what to do next.

Some turned around and caught the first steamboat to St. Michael and home. Others headed back upriver. Everyone who was leaving tried to sell his flour, oatmeal, dried fruit, and beans. Food went for a fraction of what it had cost in Seattle. Gold scales were almost worthless, since *everyone* had carried a set of scales to weigh the fortune they had expected to scoop from the streams. But the few who had brought brooms sold them for $17 apiece. And nails sold for $8 per pound.

Some pitched their tents; others camped on Dawson's waterfront in the boats they had built at Lake Bennett.

So many people living in a confined area provided a natural place for diseases to break out. Colds, influenza, measles, pneumonia, dysentery, smallpox, malaria, typhoid, and spinal meningitis were passed from one person to the next. Many died.

A Jesuit priest anticipated that with the hordes of people there would be accidents and illnesses. Father William Judge brought a sled loaded with medicine from his mission on the lower Yukon River. He convinced the miners who had struck it rich to contribute to a hospital. He worked himself to death building a hospital and tending the sick. He died of pneumonia in January 1899, but he was loved and remembered by everyone as the Saint of Dawson.

One of the early stampeders arriving in Dawson in the spring of 1897 was a woman in her twenties. Belinda Mulrooney had heard about Carmack's discovery while she was working as a stewardess on a ship in Juneau, Alaska. On her first trip to Dawson, she bought $5,000 worth of cotton clothing and hot-water bottles and headed north across Chilkoot Pass. When she arrived in Dawson, she sold the clothing and hot-water bottles for $30,000. With the profit and the help of a

Belinda Mulrooney built the Magnet Roadhouse with the help of a broken-down mule named Gerry. It is believed that the woman in the white apron is Belinda Mulrooney.

broken-down mule named Gerry, she built the first road-house, a kind of restaurant and bar, in Grand Forks.

Belinda Mulrooney (standing beside the sled) hired packers to help her get over White Pass in 1899. She brought furnishings for the Fair View Hotel: cut-glass chandeliers, plate-glass windows, fine lumber for finishing the interior, and brass bedsteads.

Mulrooney invested her money in building cabins to resell and in half a dozen mining properties. She also built the Fair View Hotel.

The Fair View's luxuries included electric lights, steam heat in twenty-two rooms, and Turkish baths. In the lobby hung a cut-glass chandelier, and the dining room was adorned with linen tablecloths, silver, china, and crystal. While a bar was at the front entrance of the hotel, the Fair View had a side entrance for ladies who did not wish to enter through the bar. According to Tappan Adney, who wrote a book about the Klondike and visited the hotel, the Fair View "possessed a bathroom."

The only thing the hotel lacked was interior walls. The rooms where people slept were divided by sheets of canvas covered with wallpaper. Anyone could hear the conversation in the next room.

Mulrooney became one of the wealthiest people in the Klondike.

The Spanish-American War had begun in February 1898, and people were eager for news. By the time newspapers arrived, they were old. One person brought a Seattle newspaper with him. A miner from Hunker Creek paid $50 for it. Then he hired "Judge" John Miller to read the paper aloud in Pioneers' Hall. Hundreds paid a dollar per person to hear the news read.

Thousands of people had endured unbelievable cold and blizzards and had moved a ton of gear across mountains and down a river. When they arrived, most did not rush to the goldfields. Instead they plodded up and down the muddy streets of Dawson, realizing that thousands had arrived before them and that the rich claims had already been staked.

When thousands of men arrived in Dawson, they realized the gold lay buried fifty feet beneath the surface on someone else's claim. With nothing better to do, they shuffled up and down Dawson's Front Street.

A few found ground to stake claims, but only a tiny percentage of those few actually found gold. Generally, going to the Klondike had not been a wise investment.

Some stayed in Dawson. There were ways to make a living without mining. They went to work for men who had good claims, or they found jobs in town. By July 1898, Dawson had two banks, two newspapers, five churches, and a local telephone service.

There were a lot of jobs and they paid well. In the United States most people made less than two dollars a day. But in Dawson a man could make ten times that weighing gold dust. Restaurant cooks earned one hundred dollars per week, and skilled carpenters were paid seventeen dollars for a ten-hour day.

Since the United States was in an economic depression, a shave and a haircut Outside would cost twenty-five cents. The same services cost five times that much in Dawson.

There was plenty of entertainment in Dawson. There were saloons and gambling halls. At the dance halls men could pay one dollar for one dance with a woman—either the Oregon Mare, Dog-face Kitty, Cheechako Lil, the Grizzly Bear, Nellie the Pig, or Diamond-Tooth Gertie. There was orchestra music or serenades by the Oatley Sisters, Lottie and Polly. One could watch Dawson's first cow get milked or watch boxing matches with Australia's heavyweight champion Frank Slavin. Or one could just walk along Front Street and point out the Klondike millionaires—Big Alex McDonald, the Lucky Swede Charlie Anderson, or Swiftwater Bill Gates.

Front Street in Dawson was much like a carnival. Stampeders could buy lemonade, peanuts, jewelry, ice cream, sausage, or fresh grapes.

There were few children in Dawson (only 163 under the age of fourteen), but a nine-year-old girl named Margie Newman was a popular stage singer.

Children attended school despite the cold, ice, and snow.

The North-West Mounted Police made sure Dawson was a law-abiding city. They kept a twelve-man police force on duty day and night.

The most serious crimes were using vile language, disorderly conduct, working on Sunday (even fishing on Sunday was against the law), and cheating. Other common crimes included dog stealing, petty thievery, and disturbing the peace. Punishment for these crimes was a fine, an order to leave town, or a sentence to chop firewood to heat government buildings. There were often as many as fifty men at a time chopping firewood for the government woodpile.

By September 1898, about 10,000 people had left Dawson to return home. The rest decided to remain at least until the spring thaw.

CHAPTER 13

---◆---

GETTING THE GOLD

Mining for gold in the Klondike was called placer mining. It was tiresome, boring, and backbreaking.

First the miners looked for gold by panning. To pan for gold, the miner scooped some sand, dirt, and gravel from the creek bottom into a gold pan that looked like a very large pie pan. He added some water, then swished the pan around and around. The lighter sand and silt would wash out over the pan's rim, leaving the gravel. Since gold is heavier than sand, it sank to the bottom. The miner sorted out the worthless gravel and then picked out the pieces of gold.

But millions of dollars in gold lay buried inside the earth. Those willing to dig beneath the surface were often rewarded. Over eons the heavy gold had washed down through the river- and streambeds and settled in pockets or crevices in the bedrock. Through the centuries, dirt and gravel had also eroded from the hillsides down into the riverbeds and covered the bedrock and the gold.

When a miner pans for gold, he finds tiny flakes that did not get buried by dirt and gravel. Even one tiny flake is called "color." Finding those tiny flakes often indicates there is a

These women try their hand at panning for gold.

larger deposit buried deeper in the earth, usually trapped in the bedrock. The miner then digs down from where he found gold in his gold pan to where the heavier, larger deposit is buried in a pocket in the bedrock. This is called "placer" mining.

Miners usually began digging in the winter. In the spring and summer the streams melted, making digging in the streams almost impossible. After the winter freeze-up, the miner wouldn't be flooded out.

The miner would dig through the frozen ground, called permafrost. The permafrost began about a foot below the surface of the soil. The miner built a fire in the hole he was digging in, an area about six feet long and four feet wide. He let the fire burn for several hours or overnight. Once the fire burned out, the miner shoveled out the layer of thawed dirt, about ten to twelve inches in depth. Then he built another fire and repeated the procedure. The dirt carried out of the hole was called muck.

As the miner dug deeper, he could no longer throw the muck out. Then he would build a windlass, which consisted of a bucket or barrel on a rope. When the bucket was filled with dirt, it was hoisted to the surface and emptied. It was helpful to have a partner so that the miner working down in the shaft didn't have to climb out every time he filled a bucket.

The worker digging in the frozen clay or rock beneath the surface was working in a small, cramped space, choking, wheezing, and gasping in the smoldering smoke from the fire. He dug to bedrock, where most of the gold lay in "pay dirt." The pay dirt was hoisted to the surface and piled in a mound known as the dump.

There was no way to tell how deep the miner would have to dig to reach bedrock. In some claims it was eight feet deep, but in others it was thirty to fifty feet below the surface. Digging the hole in the frozen ground could take a month.

Once a miner got to bedrock, he dug sideways in the direction he found the gold. This horizontal digging was called drifting. Once a miner started drifting, he usually worked lying on his back or side or in a crouched position.

At this point many miners hired help. Stampeders who arrived in Dawson after all the claims were staked were hired to do the hard work involved in getting the gold that was buried inside the earth.

When a miner dug to bedrock and found gold, he often hired help. These men are working in a shaft under number 16 on Eldorado Creek— Thomas Lippy's claim.

Sometimes a miner would get to bedrock without finding gold. That hole was called a skunk. The miner would start over and dig a new shaft. Some miners had to dig several holes. Some never found gold and abandoned their claims.

In the spring, when the creeks thawed and the water gushed, the miners scooped dirt from the dump into a sluice box. This was called the cleanup, and it was an exciting time. During cleanup, the miner could tell how much actual gold he had taken out during the winter.

A sluice was a long, narrow trough with wooden ribs or crossbars called riffles. The sluice was used on an incline. Dirt was shoveled into the sluice, then the fast-running water ran through the trough. The water washed the dirt and gravel down and out of the sluice box. The ribs or riffles caught the gold, since it was too heavy to be washed away by the water. Some gravel was also caught, so the miner had to sort out the gold by hand. About every third day, the water was stopped and the gravel at the bottom of the sluice box was panned for gold.

A young stampeder works with a gold pan and sluice box.

A rocker worked on the same general principle as a sluice box. A rocker looked somewhat like a baby's cradle—a wooden box about four feet long on rocker-shaped legs. There were holes in the bottom of the box and a shelf beneath it. The miner filled the box with dirt and gravel from the dump, then rocked it back and forth while pouring water over it. The rocking of the water caused the heavy gold to fall through the holes onto the shelf below.

The miner's life in the Klondike was difficult and boring.

Miners lived in small cabins. When a miner found a paying claim, he often took on a partner to share the work. These two men would share a cabin that was about 12 by 16 feet. A cabin 16 by 18 feet could accommodate four men.

During the long, cold winters, being confined in such small quarters often caused partners to argue. They would draw a line down the center of the cabin, and for the remainder of the winter, each man would live on his side of the line, never speaking to the other.

Two partners once took a baby moose into their cabin to raise during the winter. They got through the winter blizzards with something to keep their minds busy!

Cabins were built of logs. The roof was made of small poles placed side by side. On top of the poles was a layer of moss. On top of the moss was a foot-thick layer of clay-type earth. During the short summer, the temperature often rose to 100°F, and some cabin roofs became vegetable gardens. Radishes and turnips could be grown there. And with the heat came the mosquitoes.

Few people had real glass windows. Others used whatever they could: deerhide with the hair removed, unbleached muslin, white cotton canvas. Some people made windows

The roof of Mary's Hotel was made of moss and dirt, as were the roofs of most cabins. In the spring and summer, these roofs bloomed with wildflowers or provided fresh vegetables.

from empty bottles or jars placed on end on the windowsill and held together with mud.

Each cabin had a small table, a sleeping bunk, and sometimes a chair but usually a stool. Most of the furniture was made from tree trunks. Chairs were often wooden crates turned on end. The cabins were heated by woodstoves.

In the northlands, winter days are very short. In December daylight begins at 10:00 A.M. and the sun goes down around 2:00 in the afternoon. By 3:00 P.M. it is totally dark. In the arctic darkness, anything that provided light was valuable. An oil lamp sold for $7.50, but the coal oil to burn it was $2 to $20 per gallon (when it was available). Candles sold for $1.00 to $1.50 each.

The miners had no thermometers to tell how cold the winters were, but they had their own methods. They set four vials of liquid outside. When the vial containing mercury was frozen, they knew it was −38°F. When the vial of strong whiskey froze, they knew it was −55°F. When the vial of kerosene froze, they knew it was −65°F. And when a medicine called Perry Davis's Pain-Killer froze, they knew it was −75°F.

The valley was filled with wood smoke from the fires heating cabins and thawing the permafrost leading down to the gold deposits. The thick forest disappeared as trees were cut down to build sluice boxes, cabins, mine shafts, and cribbing. The entire Klondike region began to look like a smoldering battlefield.

CHAPTER 14

———◆◆◆———

THE END OF THE GOLD RUSH

On April 26, 1899, a fire raged through Dawson. The temperature was −45°F. Water in the canvas fire hoses froze, ripping them to shreds. The firefighters tried using dynamite to stop the spread of the fire, but even that didn't help.

The main part of the town—117 buildings—burned to the ground. Inside one bank the vault burst open, and gold nuggets, gold dust, and gold jewelry melted together into one mass.

The town was rebuilt, but it was too late. By the middle of 1899, the Klondike gold rush was over. Some stampeders who had taken the back door or other overland routes were still on the trail, still trying to get to the gold, and they wouldn't find out for months or even years that they were too late. The Klondike gold rush had lasted only three years: from Carmack's discovery in August 1896 to the summer of 1899.

All told, 100,000 stampeders had set out on the Klondike gold rush. About half arrived there. However, only 4,000 found any gold at all, and of those 4,000 only a few hundred found enough to be considered rich. A handful of those few hundred invested their money wisely. Many spent their money foolishly. Most gambled or drank it away.

In 1898 $10 million in gold was taken from the Klondike claims, and in 1899 another $16 million was taken. But in 1898 the stampeders spent $60 million to reach the Klondike.

The northlands were changed forever. Businesses moved into Alaska and the Yukon Territory. Railroads were built. Telegraphs and telephones connected the Yukon with the Outside. Laws and law enforcement were established.

A narrow-gauge railroad from Skagway over White Pass was completed to the summit by February 1899. By that time Dyea was nearly deserted and few thought it worthwhile to struggle over Chilkoot Pass.

In the summer of 1899, there were rumors that another gold discovery had been made on the beaches at Cape Nome, Alaska. Soon the rumors were confirmed. Cabins were abandoned and businesses closed in the Klondike region as prospectors boarded steamers to travel two thousand miles to the new tent city at Cape Nome.

Several hundred stampeders remained in the Yukon the rest of their lives. They worked whatever jobs were available—just so they could remain in that remote but magical place.

The men and women who rushed to the Klondike for gold were changed forever. They had achieved a goal they might never have attempted had they not been victims of gold fever.

Almost everyone who survived was a better person for the experience. As the hardships faded in their memories, they realized they had endured conditions and accomplished a feat they would never have believed possible. Each man and woman had a new sense of his or her own incredible potential.

GLOSSARY

avalanche A mass of snow, ice, rocks, and earth that suddenly slides down a mountain.

bonanza A large or rich mineral deposit.

cache A place to hide or store things like provisions.

cheechako What the natives called the newcomers.

claim A legal right to mine gold (or other minerals) on a piece of land.

color A small piece (even a single grain) of gold left in a gold miner's pan after washing.

grubstake Money advanced to a prospector to buy supplies and equipment. In return, the prospector promised to the lender a share of whatever he found.

headwaters The upper part of a stream; where a stream or river begins.

inside passage A route that goes across the interior of a country by way of land or water.

Klondike River A river that flows west across the Yukon Territory to join the Yukon River at Dawson. The river's name, given by the natives, sounded like *Thron-diuck* or *Trondiuck,* which meant "hammer-water." Every year the natives would hammer stakes into the riverbed and spread their fishing nets across the mouth of the river. Since *Thron-diuck* was difficult for the prospectors to pronounce, the name soon became Klondike.

mother lode The main vein of ore or gold in an area where many smaller veins of gold are found.

muskeg Wet, spongy ground, covered for a few miles with moss. A horse, stepping on one of these bogs, would sink to his body.

panning A method of finding gold in a stream. A prospector puts a small amount of gravel and water from a creek bed into a pan that resembles a pie pan. He swishes the mixture around, washing the lighter-weight sand over the rim of the pan. The gold, which is heavier, remains in the bottom of the pan.

placer mining A method of mining in which the deposits are found by washing or dredging underwater sand and gravel from the ore.

shell game A swindle whereby a small object is placed under one of three walnut shells. The operator moves the shells around and the bettor tries to guess which shell hides the object.

Siwash A term the prospectors gave the natives of the Yukon area. It was also a term used for anyone adopting the manners and customs of those natives.

sourdough Someone who has been a prospector in the northlands for a long time. The name comes from the prospectors' use of sourdough as a leavening for bread and pancakes.

BIBLIOGRAPHY

ADNEY, EDWIN TAPPAN. *The Klondike Stampede of 1897–98*. Fairfield, Wash.: Ye Galleon Press, 1968.

BACKHOUSE, FRANCES. *Women of the Klondike*. Vancouver/Toronto: Whitecap Books, 1995.

BECKER, ETHEL ANDERSON. *Klondike '98: Hegg's Album of the 1898 Alaska Gold Rush*. Portland, Oreg.: Binfords & Mort, Publishers, 1949.

BERTON, PIERRE. *The Golden Trail: The Story of the Klondike Rush*. Toronto: Macmillan of Canada, 1974.

———. *The Klondike Fever: The Life and Death of the Last Great Gold Rush*. New York: Alfred A. Knopf, 1965.

———. *The Klondike Quest*. Boston: Little Brown, 1983.

BRONSON, WILLIAM, with RICHARD REINHARDT. *The Last Grand Adventure*. New York: McGraw-Hill Book Company, 1977.

CLIFFORD, HOWARD. *The Skagway Story*. Anchorage, Alaska: Alaska Northwest Publishing Company, 1975.

COOPER, MICHAEL. *Klondike Fever: The Famous Gold Rush of 1898*. New York: Clarion Books, 1989.

GOUGH, BARRY M. *Gold Rush!* Toronto: Grolier, 1983.

HUNT, WILLIAM R. *North of 53°: The Wild Days of the Alaska-Yukon Mining Frontier 1870–1914*. New York: Macmillan Publishing Co., Inc., 1974.

MAYER, MELANIE J. *Klondike Women: True Tales of the 1897–98 Gold Rush*. Swallow Press/Ohio University Press, 1989.

MORGAN, MURRAY. *One Man's Gold Rush: A Klondike Album*. Seattle: University of Washington Press, 1967.

POYNTER, MARGARET. *Gold Rush! The Yukon Stampede of 1898*. New York: Atheneum, 1979.

RAY, DELIA. *Gold! The Klondike Adventure*. New York: Lodestar Books, E. P. Dutton, 1989.

SATTERFIELD, ARCHIE. *Chilkoot Pass: Then and Now*. Anchorage, Alaska: Alaska Northwest Publishing Co., 1973.

————. *Klondike Park*. Golden, Colo.: Fulcrum Publishing, 1993.

WALLACE, ROBERT. *The Old West: The Miners*. New York: Time-Life Books, 1976.

WELLS, E. HAZARD. *Magnificence and Misery: A First Hand Account of the 1897 Klondike Gold Rush*. Garden City, N.Y.: Doubleday, 1984.

WHARTON, DAVID B. *The Alaska Gold Rush*. Bloomington, Ind.: Indiana University Press, 1972.

WRIGHT, ALLEN A. *Prelude to Bonanza: The Discovery and Exploration of the Yukon*. Sidney, British Columbia: Gray's Publishing, Ltd., 1976.

Photo Credits

INDEX

Page numbers in italic type refer to illustrations.

CHARLOTTE FOLTZ JONES is the author of several highly praised works of nonfiction for children, including *Mistakes That Worked: 40 Familiar Inventions and How They Came to Be*, an IRA-CBC Children's Choice Book; *Accidents May Happen: 50 Inventions Discovered by Mistake*, A *Smithsonian* Notable Book for Children; and *Fingerprints and Talking Bones: How Real-Life Crimes Are Solved*. She lives in Boulder, Colorado.